THE
FEAST
OF OUR
LIFE

PREPARING TO **FLOURISH**
THROUGH **SELF-LOVE**

ALEJANDRO
JADAD

Beati

The Feast of Our Life: Preparing to flourish through self-love

First published in the USA by Beati Inc.

Cover by Jose Raúl Vergara (www.jv81.com)

ISBN 978-958-46-7472-2

"What is love?"

"The total absence of fear," said the Master.

"What is it we fear?"

"Love," said the Master.

Anthony de Mello (1931-1987)

Quiet words

As you read, right now, you are hearing sounds somewhere inside of your head.

These sounds - known as the inner voice – will allow me, Alex, the author who wrote these words, to engage in a special kind of conversation with you.

My intention is to establish a new kind of connection between us.

This connection will blur the boundaries among past, present and future; between here and there; between you and me; and above all, within your own self.

I became fully aware that I could hear sounds in my head back in the summer of 2007. At that time, I was trying to choose the best way to start my first non-medical book, entitled 'Unlearning'. None of the options I was considering appeared strong enough to become the frontrunner. As I weighed the pros and cons of each of the possible book beginnings, it happened!

I started to witness my own dilemmas, expressed in words that sounded like my voice, but that were not coming out of my mouth.

I could hear the words, even though they were not coming from sound waves touching my ears.

I was hearing "Me", perhaps for the first time in my life, more than 40 years after my birth!

It was a true epiphany…

The effect was so enthralling and profound, that I started to pay attention to its tone, rhythm, pitch, tempo and even volume.

As I could not find much written about it, I started to experiment with it, to push what for me were newly discovered possibilities.

Then, I decided to share some of my insights with the future readers of the book, by letting my inner voice guide them through its first chapter.

I realized that my inner voice could communicate with the inner voice of other people, just as we are doing right now.

Exhilarated, I discovered that text is perhaps the most powerful tool we humans have to transcend time and space. There, and then, I became fully aware that I could reach you here and now.

I became conscious that it did not matter whether you knew me or had heard my voice before.

It did not and does not even matter whether I am still alive.

For as long as you read this, I could communicate with you, just as I am doing now, here.

After receiving so much from so many people who are now dead, I am now using my writing to reach out to you, to share with you my journey of discovery and growth.

At the beginning, you will hear me, through your own inner voice. Gradually, as you progress through the 12 short parts in which I have divided the experience, you will notice that you are participating in a very intimate conversation.

You will find many questions along the way.

These questions might be of great value to you, as you get ready to start loving yourself, fully.

At different points, you will find some areas in Italics, like this one, which I will use to communicate directly with you.

Come along with me.

Feel free to unleash your imagination.

There is no reason to worry.

After all, nobody else will ever be able to hear us.

The story behind the story

In 2008, my best friend, Murray Enkin, asked me to help him prepare for his death. His request seemed very reasonable, given that he was about to reach his 85th birthday and had decided to declare himself old.

He, someone who had transformed childbirth worldwide, was not terminally ill. He just felt that it was time to think, talk, read and write about the process that was unfolding as he approached the end of his life, and wanted me to support him along the way.

I accepted his invitation immediately, anticipating a very exciting experience. I would act as a sounding board for him, while sharing with him as many relevant insights as possible from my experience with dying patients, and their families. I had no idea how exciting this adventure really was going to be.

During one of our initial conversations, we discovered a quote by George Santayana that gave a strong sense of direction to our maiden journey: *"There is no cure for birth and death, save to enjoy the interval".*

Soon, these words became very meaningful to me, as I found myself in hospital with a possible, albeit not probable, diagnosis of colon cancer.

Even though cancer was ruled out, facing my mortality forced me to recognize that I had spent years of my life supporting other people while they were dying, but almost no time focused on how I would like to live the rest of my own life, and even less on how I would like to die.

Suddenly, the 40-year age difference between Murray and me seemed irrelevant. It was clear that we were passengers on the same vessel, heading towards the same destination: our death. I was no longer a companion, of my patients, or of my friend. This was about me too.

What you will read from now on draws from hundreds of interactions with people I have accompanied at the end of their lives, and has been inspired by the journey I undertook as I learned how to live, while preparing for my own death.

Now is your turn to benefit from these insights, while you get ready for the feast of your life.

Love After Love

The time will come

when, with elation

you will greet yourself arriving

at your own door, in your own mirror

and each will smile at the other's welcome,

and say, sit here. Eat.

You will love again the stranger who was your self.

Give wine. Give bread. Give back your heart

to itself, to the stranger who has loved you

all your life, whom you ignored

for another, who knows you by heart.

Take down the love letters from the bookshelf,

the photographs, the desperate notes,

peel your own image from the mirror.

Sit. Feast on your life.

Derek Walcott (1930-?)

Self-love is the key

The poem Love after Love captures, beautifully, and concisely, the essence of what you will experience during this dialogue.

Its author is Derek Walcott, a poet and playwright born in St. Lucia, who received the Nobel Prize in Literature in 1992.

The poem invites us to use the power of our minds to watch ourselves participate in a very special encounter, at a very special time in the future: when we will finally meet ourselves and realize that loving our self is essential.

The mystery starts from the title. "Love" could be a noun or a verb; and "after" could mean, either at a later time or in pursuit of.

Therefore, "Love after Love" could convey, among many other possibilities, the action (love as a verb) of loving again after heartbreak, or the search for love by love.

Regardless of the intention(s), Walcott's message is clearly a call for us to wake up to a wonderful opportunity: we must, could and should aspire to experience deep, unrestricted, unquestionable, unconditional self-love.

Self-love is rarely addressed positively.

In most cultures, particularly those with a strong Judeo-Christian influence, it is considered virtuous to love others, but sinful to love oneself. It is assumed that loving is a zero-sum game; if one loves oneself, it detracts from loving others.

Self-love, therefore, is equated with selfishness and egotism. Religious leaders, such as Calvin, regarded self-love as a "noxious pest", while St. Augustine considered it as "the primal destruction of man".

On closer inspection, however, selfishness and self-love, rather than synonyms, could actually be opposites. A selfish person does not care about others. Self-love depends on and enriches the lives of others. The Bible, in fact, urges us to love our neighbour as we love ourselves. This is considered to be The Greatest Commandment. Inevitably, it is impossible to love others unless we love us first; the more we love ourselves, the more we could love others.

If it is a virtue to love my neighbour as a human being, it is also a virtue to love myself. After all, I am a human being too.

Walcott appears to have understood this well, when he brings up bread and wine, such powerful Christian symbols, immediately after reassuring us that we will love our self again. Practically all religions and ethical systems in the world follow variations of a similar precept, known as The Golden Rule, which could be summarized as "Do to others what you would like them to do to you".

The poet also shows us that 15 lines are enough to display a deep understanding of human nature and to give us an epic poem.

He knows, clearly, that we have the capacity to use our minds to watch ourselves, as if we were participating in an out of body experience. This ability, which psychologists call "self-reflection" is one of the most powerful tools we humans have to shape our selves, and to change our lives.

For years, it was believed that our actions were a reflection of our personality and attitudes. For instance, if we have a generous nature, we would engage in volunteer work or give money to charity.

Hundreds of studies indicate that this works also in the reverse order; we humans often need to look to our own behaviour to figure out who we are.

Therefore, we judge who we are, to a large extent, by reflecting upon what we do. If we do volunteer work or donate money, for example, we would conclude that we are generous.

This is the basis for behavioural-cognitive therapy, which operates in reverse from the better-known cognitive-behavioural approach.

Walcott also knows that our minds can travel in time.

We have the capacity to imagine scenarios of the future, experience them vividly, and remember them later on, particularly when they are positive.

He also seems to be aware of theories that suggest that, rather than one person, there are many co-existing inside ourselves, all with different and competing desires, attitudes and preferences. In keeping with this view, which has been held by leading thinkers since antiquity, Walcott speaks to us using the second person singular. He opens the poem by bringing together two versions of us ("you" and "yourself"), as equals, and invites them to greet each other. "You", in proper grammatical fashion, is the subject of the poem, receiving from the author instructions on how to fall in love again with the other, who is addressed as "the stranger" and "your self".

The last stanza is a call to action that evokes Pagan, pre-Christian, times. In just three lines, the poet commands us, categorically, to become one whole person, again, and to turn our life into a joyful banquet.

Thanks to this beautiful, complete, poem, we should look forward to reaching that day, when we will hail that who we must love above all others: our self. Perhaps, that day we will discover that all we needed to feast on our lives, and to flourish in every possible way, was to re-learn how to listen.

Then, we will never be, or feel, lonely again.

Greeting yourself

Listen

"I am alive like you, and I am standing beside you. Close your eyes and look around, you will see me in front of you..."

Khalil Gibran (1883 -1931)

Do you hear me?

Reading, just like thinking or dreaming, allows me to come to life.

Some call me "The Inner Voice". Others call me "Inner Speech".

Can you hear me, clearly, now?

What am I?

Who am I?

Am I one, or many?

Nobody knows.

You are not even sure whether I sound like your own voice.

Am I text?

Am I sound?

Am I both?

Am I neither?

It really does not matter.

Many are trying to figure this out.

They might come up with an answer.

They might not.

I might remain a mystery, forever.

I am inviting you to be part of the most important intimate conversation you would ever have. It will be strange, as it involves only one voice, one person and several points of view.

How could this be?

Because **I am whom you have always called "Me"**.

Observe

"Awake. Be the witness of your thoughts."

The Dhammapada (as translated by Tom Byrom)

Where do I come from?

Pay attention…

Listen to "Me", carefully.

I seem to come from some place inside your head, behind your eyes…

You cannot silence me on purpose.

I go silent only when you are sleeping, under anaesthesia, in coma or dead.

I am your experiencing self.

I am the one who judges.

I am the one who reflects.

The one who makes plans.

The one who trusts and falls in love.

The one who makes you feel that you exist.

Some think that your brain and your mind have created me (or should I say, "Me"?) to place you, and everything you feel, at the centre of the world.

Others believe that I have been created to fill your life with purpose, meaning and significance.

I can also fill you with sorrow, doubt, regret and terror.

Just like your eyes cannot see themselves, I am the part of you that experiences but cannot experience itself.

I am the only solution to your most challenging riddle: How to describe yourself to your Self.

You are whom you have always called, "I".

Visualize

"Is all that we see or seem but a dream within a dream?"

Edgar Allan Poe (1809-1849)

Who are "you", the one you call "I"?

You are the one others can see.

You are the one who others can hear.

You are the one others call by your name.

You are the one who can see others, the one who can listen to them.

The one who can touch them; the one who can call them by name.

You can smell the roses, and feel the wind on your body. You can taste. You are the point of view from which you view the world.

You are the perceiving one.

You give me life.

You are the only one who can hear me.

I make you think. I shape you.

Would you like to see me?

Stand in front of a mirror.

Can you see past the reflection?

Close your eyes.

Can WE sense a whole person?

Can WE recognize the stranger who has loved us all our life?

Can WE welcome the only person only you and I can call our "Self"?

Engage

"We know so little about one another. We embrace a shadow and love a dream."

Hjalmar Söderberg (1869–1941)

We started building a story almost from the moment we were born.

You have contributed what you see, hear, touch, taste and smell every instant we are awake.

I have responded to those feelings, aided by our memories, by adding a sense of consistency and stability, that gives you comfort. I have made us feel real.

What we recognize as our "Self", our own life, might be the most powerful illusion created by our mind.

We believe that we are a person, with our own identity.

We believe that we have our own emotions, desires, points of view, roles, beliefs and values, for as long as we are alive.

At the same time, our life is relentlessly evolving.

We pay a lot of attention, and respond, to feedback from ourselves and from others.

We are constantly watching and trying to understand our emotions, the expectations of other people and what is happening around us.

We are constantly trying to conform.

This could go on for as long as we live.

We are at risk of being always unfinished.

Perhaps we should remain unfinished.

This is why it is so important to take a break, right now.

Let's reflect upon what we would like to be.

Let's look at ourselves, anew.

Let's surprise ourselves by how much we can imagine.

The preparation

Imagine

"We are what we pretend to be, so we must be careful about what we pretend to be."

Kurt Vonnegut (1922-2007)

What would we do if we could do anything we like?

What would we ask the Genie of the Magic Lamp if we could only ask one wish?

What would we do if money were no barrier?

What kind of life would we like to live if we could do anything we want, right now?

Who do we really desire to be?

What would we do if we had no fear?

Let's ponder these questions.

They should help us focus our attention on what is truly important to us, to our Self, to our life.

Let's not rush to answer.

There may not be clear answers.

Let's just free our imagination.

Let's picture in our mind a new "we", a new "I", a new "Me", and a new "Self".

Let's dream of a new reality for our life.

What elements of the dream reside inside of what we consider as our Self?

Which elements are "out there", in what we perceive as the external world?

What would it take to make the dream real?

What could we do on our own to make it happen?

Who do we need to bring on board as support?

Support

"There are seeds of self-destruction in all of us that will bear only unhappiness if allowed to grow."

Dorothea Brande (1893-1948)

At times, we need help.

At times, we are our worst enemy.

Is there anyone who could hurt us more than ourselves?

Who could fool us more than ourselves?

Could we really protect our Self from ourselves?

What if we considered self-love to be a plural term?

What if we had committed travel companions through life, ready to lend us a hand, an ear or a shoulder when we feel most vulnerable and lonely?

Who are our main co-conspirators, our accomplices?

Who are those who love us more than we deserve?

Who should we approach?

Who could and should be aware of our dreams and nightmares?

Who should be empowered enough to tell us what we need to hear, not just what we want to hear?

Who will be by our side at the scariest moments?

Who do we really trust?

The SACRED journey

Protection

How could one know whether we are making decisions that would enable us to live a full life?

As I reflected upon this at the beginning of my own journey, it became clear that I had more than one inner voice, competing for attention, and emerging from different levels of awareness.

Right now, for instance, you will recognize one that is produced while you read these words, one that analyzes them, and yet another who is examining the other two.

When I focused on my own trustworthiness, as to my capacity to love my Self, I discovered several "Mes" competing for dominance. Some were unpleasant (e.g., "Fearful Alex", "Insensitive Alex"), while others were more self-loving ("Pleasure-seeking Alex", "Generous Alex"), and a few in between.

If this was the case for me, it was bound to be the same for anyone else.

Rather than becoming paralyzed by this startling discovery, I developed a plan for protection, from myself and others, which seemed to work well.

I chose people who had their interests aligned with those of my most self-loving "Mes": Martha, my wife; Alia and Tamen, our daughters; and relatives by choice, my closest friends and mentors.

I invited them to join my Personal Board of Directors. Their main task would be to give me their opinion about how I was living my life, and to give me suggestions and specific goals as to how to improve, explicitly and at regular intervals.

I then took their views, suggestions and goals as elements to inform and guide the conversation among my multiple voices.

This allowed me, at last, to be able to press the pause button, and reflect, confidently, on how to live a healthy and happy life, full of love, and with no regrets, until my last breath.

This approach might also be valuable to you, as your own adventure unfolds.

Before you proceed, try to answer:

Who should be a member of your Personal Board of Directors?

Stop

"I suggest we intervene on our own behalf – and that we do it right now, in the present moment. When things begin accelerating wildly out of control, sometimes patience is the only answer. Press pause. We have time for this."

Douglas Rushkoff (1961-?)

Let's be honest with each other.

We are not fully aligned yet.

You and I have been separated from each other for a long time.

We are not a "we" yet.

What I think and what you say are often very different.

What you say rarely agrees with what I expect you to do.

I should be blamed for our separation.

When you were asked to do as you were told, to conform, I failed to give you the courage to refuse. I made you feel weak and vulnerable.

I knew that all you had to say was, "No!" to break the spell. Instead of making it obvious, safe or easy, I made you feel insecure. I allowed fear to conquer us.

What deserves such a "No!" now?

Are we truly prepared to love our self unconditionally?

Are we prepared to put our sources of joy and peace of mind at the top of our priorities?

Do we feel that loving our Self is a form of narcissism, egotism or selfishness?

What if now, just like passengers of a plane that is decompressing, we decided to put our oxygen mask on first, breathe deeply, and gather strength?

What is preventing us from helping our Self before we help others?

Are we – those we call "I", "Me", "my Self" - prepared to accept that the only way to love others fully is to love **our** Self fully?

What would it take for us to work, and flourish together.

It is time for us to align.

Align

"Ultimately, the reason why love and compassion bring the greatest happiness is simply that our nature cherishes them above all else."

Tenzin Gyatso, the 14th Dalai Lama (1950-?)

Becoming one will only happen if your incentives and mine are in sync.

What if you and I could identify a common, seemingly unreachable goal that we would value above all others?

Is there a goal that neither you nor I could reach alone?

What if we focused on what humans have regarded for millennia as the ultimate objective of any existence – a good, full life?

What if we discovered, uncovered and recovered our own abilities to harmonize what we feel, what we think, what we say and what we do?

We cannot afford to diverge.

What if we began by identifying our most cherished feeling, and used it to line up our thoughts, words and actions?

The wait will be worthwhile.

What feeling would we like to experience more often than any other?

What makes Me happiest? What gives Me the greatest feeling of emotional wellbeing?

What is <u>Your</u> verb? What action would you like to perform more than any other?

It might take us a while to answer these questions.

We must be urgently patient.

The beaming smile

When my father died of lung cancer in 2002, three years after the death of my maternal grandfather, I became aware of yet another important fact: **I was next.**

I also realized that most people were dying of complications of multiple chronic incurable diseases, which had become the main killer of humans since the late 20th century.

I started to notice that there was a lot of unnecessary suffering at the end of life as a result of isolation and loneliness, poorly managed symptoms, loss of independence and social neglect.

This grim picture compelled me to devote the rest of my professional life to enabling people to make the most of whatever time they had left to live.

Soon, I discovered that we had lots of data about where people die and when, but almost no knowledge about how we die, and even less about how we would like to die.

I started to ask patients and loved ones about how they would like to live the rest of their days, only to realize that it was the first time for most of them to think about it.

To facilitate the discussions, I would ask them about what made them happiest in life, and to identify "their verb". Most people, interestingly, would give a blank look and produce the answers almost immediately. Consistently, they would tell me with a very ample grin. Then, we would develop a plan to ensure that they could conjugate their verb as much and as often as possible, to secure maximum joy and peace of mind until the end.

Most of the time, we wished this process could have started much earlier in life.

In 2008, when I had my cancer false alarm, I realized that I had not asked myself what made me happiest, and that I had not made efforts to identify my own verb.

It took me three months, and many attempts, to produce the radiant smile I had seen in my patients.

My conclusion: I am happiest when I do not know, when I face uncertainty, the unknown. My verb is to question, or more precisely, to wonder.

This realization had a huge impact on my life. It empowered me to align what I feel, think, say and do during each day and hour I am awake.

As I enjoyed progressively long periods of bliss and serenity with an intensity that I thought was unreachable or unrealistic, I started to ask the two questions to my family members, my closest friends and co-workers.

Knowing what gives us the greatest and most intense joy, and our verbs, has turned us into enthusiastic accomplices, committed to helping each other conjugate them as often as possible, to achieve maximum emotional wellbeing, without regrets.

Now it is your turn, if you choose to try.

What makes you happiest?

What is your verb?

Chart

"Find out where joy resides, and give it a voice far beyond singing. For to miss the joy is to miss all."

Robert Louis Stevenson (1850-1894)

Now, we must think and act like ancient mapmakers trying to make sense of an unknown world.

We will be facing an uncharted territory: the rest of our life.

We know the voyage starts here and now. We do not know when it will end.

But it will end. One day, sooner than we think, we will die.

What if our mission is not to reach a specific destination, but to get the best navigational tools to guide the journey from now until our last breath?

What if our purpose is not to create a definite version of the unique map of our life?

What if, instead, we looked at each hour we live as a **"life unit"**?

What if we truly believed that there is nothing more important to us than to enjoy each of them, conjugating our verb, doing what we love most?

What if joyful tranquility became our compass?

What if our only boundary is harm to others?

What if, purposefully, we enabled others to identify what makes them happiest?

What if we invited others to discover their verbs?

What if we started with those in our support team?

How far would we go if we knew that, together with our trusted companions, we could push the boundaries of what we have considered possible until now?

What if we, our Self and those closest to us, joined forces and decided to overcome, once and for all, all of the obstacles we must remove?

Remove

"My life has been full of terrible misfortunes most of which never happened."

Michel de Montaigne (1533-1592)
[Often attributed also to Mark Twain (1835-1910)]

I have been sabotaging us all our life.

I have enabled terrible forces to overpower us, to paralyze us. I have collected sorrows, putting them on our shoulders, like rocks in a backpack, all our life.

I bring some rocks from the past. They are the heaviest, and mostly made of REGRETS. They are full of "should haves" and "could haves". They nibble at us from the inside.

Do we feel guilty or ashamed for having hurt someone? What can we do to seek forgiveness or make amends?

Are there things we wish we had done but did not do? Can we do them now?

I bring other rocks from the present. They are very tiring, as they are made of FRUSTRATION. They are full of negative "whys" and "why nots" that drain us from the outside, particularly when others do not meet our expectations.

I bring other rocks from the future. They are the most paralyzing, as they are made of FEAR, of pain, of becoming vulnerable, of failure, of embarrassment, of not meeting our basic needs, and above all, of our own death. They are full of catastrophic "what ifs" and "what nexts".

What is the worst that can happen?

What if we have no control over the future?

What if we are at the mercy of chance, with little room for us to change what will happen?

What if, instead of chasing happiness, while trying to change the actual events in our life or control the future, we focused on modulating how we perceive them and how we respond to them?

What if we could cultivate calm indifference to negative thoughts and experiences, while we do what we love, as the best strategy to a full life?

What if we could eliminate all of our burdens, and felt free to explore?

Explore

"Come dress yourself in love, let the journey begin."

Francesca da Rimini
[Australian artist, with an unknown birth date]

Now, we must prepare the feast of our life.

We must prepare to love our self unconditionally, despite (or even because) our flaws.

What would we choose if the menu included anything that gives us pleasure?

What would be our first choice?

How far would we go if our only limit would be not to harm others?

What would we do if forgiveness, sin and salvation were irrelevant?

What if, instead of focusing on what we think we want, we focused on what we love?

We have tasted it already.

What would we live for?

What should be non-negotiable?

How would we really enjoy spending the rest of our life?

What if, by figuring this out, we could become a whole authentic person, at last?

What if, once we discovered our path to liberation, we decided to share with the world who we truly are, and decided to debut?

Debut

"Let the beauty of what you love be what you do."

Rumi (1207-1273)

We did not choose to be born when and where we did.

We did not choose this society with its rules and institutions.

We did not choose our family.

What if we could re-emerge into the world, on purpose?

What if we could live only on our own terms?

What if we were free to say, "No, thanks!" to anything or anybody we do not like?

How would we feel, sound and look if we were a whole person, full of life, aligned and free?

What if we were free to be surrounded only by people we love and who love us in return?

How would it feel to be free to assist others, when we feel like it?

What if we were free to accept that we are insignificant, and laugh about the cares of the world?

How would it feel to accept that nothing really matters, except what we choose to matter?

What if we were free to accept our mortality, understanding that death gives meaning to life?

What if we were free to choose serenity above all?

Free to enjoy this.

Free to enjoy here.

Free to enjoy now.

Amen!

Freedom

After three years, Murray and I reached several important conclusions.

The first one was that we are not important at all. As individuals, not even our own descendants will remember us in four or five generations. Try it with your own ancestors. Would you be able to say something about any of your 16 great, great grand parents, or any of your 32 great, great, great grand parents? Even though you exist thanks to them, they are gone, unknown, forever. The same will happen to you, if you have children. You will be gone in a few years, unknown, forever.

As a species, we will be extinct at some point, be it in five years, 50, 500, 5,000 or 5,000,000.

We also realized that we have the ability to value things and experiences at will, even when we know that they are intrinsically worthless. We learn this from an early age, when we bet beans as children, and keep doing it into adulthood, when we use chips at a casino, or when we accept that paper money, or even bytes, can purchase goods.

In addition, we recognized our capacity to suspend our disbelief at will. This is obvious when we are moved to tears or experience terror by a movie or a play, knowing full well that we have paid for a seat at the theatre.

Finally, we concluded that, for as long as we felt well, the only real option we had was to stay alive. We did not want to kill ourselves or needed to do so. Therefore, it was very important for us to determine how best to live the rest of our lives.

Putting all of these conclusions together, we hypothesized that even though we knew that nothing was important, we would be able to give importance to people, places and things at will, in such a way that we could create experiences that would give us maximum joy, with no regrets.

We also formulated the alternative hypothesis: whenever something bothered us, we could have the capacity to suspend our belief and render it unimportant, so that it would not be able to cause suffering.

In sum, we learned that nothing really matters, apart from what matters to us. Therefore, we must be very careful as to what we choose to matter to us.

We engaged in lots of thought experiments and played with different situations that presented during our activities of daily living. After a while, we found that we could create and engage in joyful experiences that were very calming, or to erase or detach from situations that started to produce negative emotions in us.

Finally, we decided that we could use our newfound skill to become characters in an enjoyable and meaningful story that we would try to make last until our deaths.

We now hope that this intimate conversation would help you prepare for the creation of your own story, and that you would soon be able to feast on your life.

Yours,

All the Alexes

About the Author

Alex is a physician, educator, entrepreneur, researcher, public advocate, and healer. His mission is to enable individuals, communities and organizations, anywhere, to experience healthy and happy lives, full of love, with no regrets, until the last breath.

He has been called a "human Internet", as his research and innovation work seeks to identify and connect the best minds, the best knowledge and the best tools across traditional boundaries to eliminate unnecessary suffering, and to imagine, create and promote new and better approaches to human flourishing across the world, as passengers of a sustainable planet.

For more information about Alex, visit https://en.wikipedia.org/wiki/Alejandro_R._Jadad_Bechara

Thanks

To those who shared so many joys, fears and wise insights during the last days of their lives.

To those whose comments improved this text substantially: Martha Garcia, Alia and Tamen Jadad-Garcia, Juan David Vergara, Andrew Sofocli, Randi Fiat, Barbara Groth, Svjetlana Kovacevic, Anita McGahan, Ashita Mohapatra, Jeff Teal and Murray Enkin.

To your "I", your "Me" and your "Self" for engaging in this most intimate conversation, and for accepting the invitation to the feast of our life.